PREFACE

This short daily devotional was created from an idea that was dropped in my heart by the Holy Spirit to encourage the daughters of God. Many of us wear numerous hats, whether it's being a wife, mother, sister, friend, aunt, etc. It's easy for us to get lost in the roles we play. I felt the heart of the Father wanting to remind us of our identity in Him and ultimately His love for us.

This devotional differs from the outline of a general devotional, but I still attribute it to be classified as one, as each scripture and "love note" of the day compels you to meditate on His Word while magnifying His presence in your daily life.

The devotional is 28 days as I intentionally released it in the month of February; what society deems as the love month by widely recognizing Valentine's Day. My prayer is that the heart of every reader will be touched by the heart of the Father, and each "love-note" reaffirms who you are in Him.

"Before I formed you in the womb I knew you, before you were born I set you apart; I appointed you as a prophet to the nations."

Jeremiah 1:5 (NIV)

THE DEPTH OF YOUR BEING IS INTRICATELY WOVEN BY ME

Day 1

"My frame was not hidden from you when I was being made in secret, intricately woven in the depths of the earth."
Psalms 139:15 (ESV)

The extent of who you are lies beyond the surface and the resemblance of your earthly family. When I created you, I was intentional about every thread and fiber woven together to form you. With careful thought, I sculpted the depths of your very being. In the stillness and silence my hand held your frame.

Even while in the darkness I saw you from afar. Don't you for a second think I rushed your making. I designed you with care and intention. You question your substance and the essence of who you are, if only you could see what I do. For the depths of your being lie within your core. Although some may never have the pleasure of knowing what lies beyond the surface, may you rest in the confidence of being designed with precision and purpose.

***Prayer**: Father, I thank you for the depth of who I am was intricately woven by you. You designed me just the way I am. May I embrace whom you have created me to be. When this world persuades me to blend in or even agree with an identity that you did not design for me; may your Word quicken me that the depths of my being were designed with precision, and purpose and executed well. I am enough. In Jesus' name, Amen.*

My Heart Note

(Take this time to write any note of reflection, personal takeaway, or note to the Father)

YOU WERE CREATED WITH CARE AND ATTENTION

Day 2

"I praise you because I am fearfully and wonderfully made; your works are wonderful; I know that full well."
Psalms 139:14 (NIV)

As the Creator and giver of life, I delight myself in my creation. While I have formed and created many things I have fashioned humankind into my likeness, and as a great sculptor I have specifically formed you. There isn't any other person that has anything like your design; you are one of a kind. Exclusively and delightfully constructed, I reverently sculpted your being. As I sit back and look at you, my creation, my daughter, I am still in awe, I rejoice at your creation. Though you may struggle with the acceptance of being brilliantly crafted in my image in a world that values superficiality, may you find reassurance that my works and how I formed you is perfect.

***Prayer**: Father, I thank you for creating me with care and attention for I am fearfully and wonderfully made. In the moments where I question my value and my worth, may I be quieted by your love and your thoughts toward me. You created me for this very moment, and may I rest knowing that in everything you do, you do well, including creating me. In Jesus' name, Amen.*

My Heart Note

(Take this time to write any note of reflection, personal takeaway, or note to the Father)

YOU ARE A NEW CREATION IN CHRIST

Day 3

"Therefore, if anyone is in Christ, he is a new creation. The old has passed away; behold, the new has come."
2 Corinthians 5:17 (ESV)

When you came to me and accepted Jesus as your Lord and your Savior the life you've lived up to that moment died and your new life in me begun. In the newness of life, you now live unto me and not just to yourself. I breathed new life into you by my Holy Spirit to empower you to live for righteousness. Your old nature, hinged on 'self' has been crushed and dissolved by my nature that now governs you. Does this mean you're perfect? No, but it does mean you can confidently live through me, the perfect one. With each passing day, you are being transformed more into my likeness as the new creation that you are. May you walk freely in the newness of life in me with the garments of grace, joy, and peace that I have clothed you with.

***Prayer**: Father, I thank you that I am a new creation in Christ Jesus. I no longer live to my flesh. The old man has died, and my new life in you has begun. I live now through the spirit and in the newness of life. I am no longer sin consciousness but God-conscious. All things have become new. In Jesus' Name, Amen*

My Heart Note

(Take this time to write any note of reflection, personal takeaway, or note to the Father)

YOUR LIFE HAS PURPOSE

Day 4

"For I know the plans I have for you, declares the Lord, plans for welfare, and not for evil, to give you a future and a hope."
Jeremiah 29:11(ESV)

From the moment I created you, I gave you purpose; I predestined my plans for your life designed to give you hope and a future; so when the moments in life provoked you to question the value or intent of it, you would find rest in my words of certainty that your life has a purpose. My daughter, if only you could see. As my plans for you unfold and through the adversity, cares, and burdens of this life, may you know that my plan for you is still good, even when you don't understand and even question my love for you. My precious daughter, you are mine, and my intentions are never to harm you, to hurt you, or to destroy you. Know that I am good, my thoughts toward you are good, and my plan for you is good.

***Prayer**: Father, I thank you that my life has purpose; even when it's hard to see your hand and it's hard to believe. May my soul find rest in your word that you know the plans you have for my life and they are good and not evil. Give me your eyes Father in times when my vision is clouded by the uncertainty and challenges of this life. I receive your peace now over my life that through you I have hope and you have given me an expected end that is good. In Jesus Name, Amen*

My Heart Note

(Take this time to write any note of reflection, personal takeaway, or note to the Father)

YOU ARE ARMED WITH STRENGTH

Day 5

"God arms me with strength, and he makes my way perfect."
Psalms 18:32 (NLT)

There are moments within your season that you will have to fight; you will have to engage in warfare against the lies of the enemy. I know at times you may feel overwhelmed, running on fumes, and consumed by the intensity of the battle. However, I never intended for you to carry the load of it all or to fight alone. I have empowered you through my Holy Spirit to engage in strategic warfare by giving you instruction and counsel along your path. I have clothed you with courage, fortitude, and endurance. I have armed you with strength for the journey. Pull from my strength my daughter and you will find rest for your soul.

***Prayer**: Father, I thank you that you have armed me with strength. I surrender every burden; roll every care and draw from the strength that you have empowered me with through your Spirit. In my weakness, your strength is made perfect. I receive your counsel as you make my way perfect before me. In Jesus' Name, Amen.*

My Heart Note

(Take this time to write any note of reflection, personal takeaway, or note to the Father)

YOU ARE REDEEMED

Day 6

"Do not fear. I have redeemed you. I have summoned you by name. You are mine." Isaiah 43:1 (NIV)

Just as I have saved you from your sin, you have the promise of my salvation. The ransom has been paid, you have been set free from every penalty of sin and from the hand of every foe. You have been released from blame, condemnation, and accusation, though the enemy will try to convince you otherwise. You have been restored in me my daughter, so live your life free of condemnation but in surrender to me. Allow my words to fill your mouth, allow what I say become what you say. Let those redeemed saay so...you are redeemed my daughter, say so.

***Prayer**: Father, I thank you that I have redemption through you. For you have redeemed me from the curse of the law and I no longer live under the law but under grace. I thank you for your redemptive power that has saved me from the penalty of sin. I thank you that my sins are forgiven, and I live my life free from the enslavement of condemnation but in freedom in you. In Jesus name, Amen.*

My Heart Note

(Take this time to write any note of reflection, personal takeaway, or note to the Father)

YOU ARE NOT ABANDONED, BUT ADOPTED

Day 7

"God decided in advance to adopt us into his own family by bringing us to himself through Jesus Christ. This is what he wanted to do, and it gave him great pleasure."
Ephesians 1:5 (NLT)

In moments where you feel alone, overlooked, rejected, abandoned, and neglected by the ones you love; may your heart find comfort in knowing that I have chosen you. It gave me great delight to choose you and adopt you into my family as my daughter. I predestined to have you as my own. You were not an afterthought, for I was intentional about my desire for you from the very beginning. Why do you still question my love for you? You are the one I chose, and because you are my child, you are my heir and co-heir with Christ; everything I have, belongs to you as well.

Prayer: *Father, I thank you that you have adopted me into your family through Christ Jesus. I am not abandoned or an orphan, but I am your daughter and a co-heir with Christ. Help me to live through a place of sonship for I am no longer a slave. I live in a place of abundance and not lack or need, because everything belongs to you; because I am your child, I have full rights to your inheritance. In Jesus' name, Amen.*

My Heart Note

(Take this time to write any note of reflection, personal takeaway, or note to the Father)

YOU ARE JOINED TO ME

Day 8

"But the one united with the Lord
is one spirit with him."
1 Corinthians 6:17 (NET)

My daughter, your mind, will, and emotions (soul) often try to overshadow the truth that you are joined to me. I am not joined to your soul, nor do I operate through your soul, but through your spirit. It is through the death and resurrection of Jesus Christ that you may serve in newness of spirit. Because you are joined to me you do not live this life alone. In me and through me you can overcome the world, because I already have. My spirit is life-giving and because you are joined to me, your spirit cannot be hindered or disturbed by anything on this earth. Do not fret; live in the newness of life through my spirit that is joined to yours. I, the Greater One lives inside of you.

***Prayer**: Father, I thank you that I am united in spirit with you. I thank you that you, the Greater One, lives on the inside of me and I am now able to live from a place of victory and not defeat. Father, help me to live in the newness of life that only your Spirit can give. I surrender myself, my way, and my will to yours. I command my flesh to submit to my spirit man that I may do your will. In Jesus' name, Amen.*

My Heart Note

(Take this time to write any note of reflection, personal takeaway, or note to the Father)

YOU HEAR MY VOICE AND YOU'RE GUIDED BY IT

Day 9

"Whether you turn to the right or to the left, your ears will hear a voice behind you, saying 'This is the way; walk in it."
Isaiah 30:21(KJV)

I have designed a purpose for your journey. There will be paths straightway, hills, turns, valleys, and plateaus. However, wherever your feet shall tread my voice will lead the way. In a world full of voices, fear, and uncertainty often shout the loudest. But as you listen to my still small voice; never forceful, hasty, or insensitive, you will find safety in my leading. For I am guiding your every footstep as your protector, defender, and sustainer. Why do you fear? I know stepping into the unknown can be unsettling but I did not give you a spirit of fear but of power, love, and a sound mind. Heed my voice, I will not cause your feet to stumble and fall.

***Prayer**: Father, I thank you that you are the great Shepherd and as your sheep, I hear your voice, and the voice of a stranger I will not follow. Whether I turn to the right or the left, your voice is there to guide me and your presence is with me. I will not fear. I submit to your leadership and your guidance. Not in front or behind but I am walking in line with your voice. Give me strength for the journey and may I learn to trust you even when I can't see my way, but may I rest in knowing that you can. In Jesus' name. Amen.*

My Heart Note

(Take this time to write any note of reflection, personal takeaway, or note to the Father)

YOU ARE NO LONGER BOUND BUT FREE

Day 10

"For freedom, Christ has set us free. Stand firm, then, and do not be subject again to the yoke of slavery."
Galatians 5:1(NRSV)

The life you live now is found in me. You were once bound to the yoke and bondage of religious servitude but through Christ, you have been set free. Do not become ensnared with the lies of the enemy that that yoke still belongs to you. The burden of religion is not your portion (the burden to serve out of obligation, rules, and restrictions that the law brings). You are no longer under the law but under grace! May you now serve me out of relationship and in the freedom of Christ Jesus. Stand strong in the freedom that has been provided and do not take on the yoke of slavery again my daughter.

***Prayer**: Father, I thank you that the life I live is found in you; my freedom is in you. I am no longer bound but I am free. Father, help me to continue to serve you out of that freedom, and when the urge to serve you out of works comes and try to enslave me to the yoke of servitude, may I be reminded that is not by my works but by your grace. I serve you through faith and I receive your grace in Jesus' name, Amen.*

My Heart Note

(Take this time to write any note of reflection, personal takeaway, or note to the Father)

YOU ARE NOT IGNORED BUT HEARD

Day 11

"In my distress, I called upon the Lord, and cried out to my God; He heard my voice from His temple, and my cry came before Him, even to His ears."

Psalms 18:6 (NIV)

My daughter, I understand on this journey it may yield tears. Tears of anguish, pain, affliction, and heaviness. Whether they are audible tears or cries of the heart; I your Father, hears. You are never overlooked, passed over, or discarded. There will be moments that in your time of distress no one will be near or may even turn a deaf ear; may you know that I am always near, waiting for you to come to me. There is no cry that doesn't touch me. There's no grief too big or small that produces a tear that I won't catch. My daughter, I have collected every tear in a bottle and recorded each one in my book.

***Prayer**: Father, I thank you that you are a God that hears. You have commanded me to cry out to you and you will answer me. When I call your name, you will respond. I thank you father that I am not ever ignored but you hear my voice. In Jesus' Name. Amen.*

My Heart Note

(Take this time to write any note of reflection, personal takeaway, or note to the Father)

YOU ARE MORE THAN A CONQUEROR

Day 12

"Yet in all these things we are more than conquerors through Him who loved us."
Romans 8:37 (AMP)

Because I have already gone before you, I know how this end. My daughter, victory has already been attained. The enemy will have you feeling like you're defeated but the truth is, that battle was already fought on your behalf and the victory has come through Jesus. Therefore, because you are mine, you share in that victory and are deemed a victor. Pick your head up. No accusation or judgment from dark forces against you can stand. The victory is now and forever more. I cause you to triumph. You don't have to strive to be victorious, you already are. Walk as such my daughter.

***Prayer**: Father, I thank you that I am a victor through Christ Jesus. I am not defeated, but I have the victory. May I remember this in times of adversity when my circumstances and situation look helpless. I look to you as the author and finisher of my faith, you've have gone before me and the battle is won. In Jesus name, Amen.*

My Heart Note

(Take this time to write any note of reflection, personal takeaway, or note to the Father)

YOU HAVE THE MIND OF CHRIST

Day 13

"For who has understood the mind of the Lord so as to instruct him?" But we have the mind of Christ." 1 Corinthians 2:16 (ESV)

As you have come into the knowledge of me, by my Spirit you are able to access my thoughts to think how I think and to see the spiritual aspect of things. I have given you power through my spirit to understand the revelation that comes from Me. There will be those around you that aren't able to comprehend the spiritual things for they have not come into the knowledge of me; they are walking as blind men. May your light conitune to shine before them my daughter.

***Prayer**: I thank you Father that I have the mind of Christ and therefore I am confident in your voice and how you feel toward me. Help me Father to share your love and thoughts you have toward those who are in need of it. In Jesus' Name, Amen.*

My Heart Note

(Take this time to write any note of reflection, personal takeaway, or note to the Father)

YOU ARE WORTH IT,NOT WORTHLESS

Day 14

"For God so loved the world, that he gave his only Son, that whoever believes in him should not perish but have eternal life."
John 3:16 (KJV)

In the moments that you feel like you're not enough... even in the moments where you feel like you are worthless, may my love flood your heart at the remembrance that I gave my only begotten son for you. I chose you in the beginning of time. My choice of choosing you was not predicated that you would ever choose me, or believe on me, but my choice was centered on my deep love for you my daughter. My love for you is not based on what you do for me. My love for you existed long before I called you to be. Yes people will come in and out of your life, some will only be there for their gain; but it's in no way a reflection of your worth; they simply do not have the capacity to see the beauty and depth of my creation, YOU. You are valuable you are worth it, not worthless.

***Prayer**: Father, I thank you for creating me. I am valuable and my worth is not contingent on how others see me, or even how I see myself, but how you see me. May you give me your eyes in the moments I feel worthless, so that I may see who I really am. May I find value in my design, whom you created. I silence every voice that speaks contrary to what you say about me, by saying what you say about me. I am not worthless, but I am worth it. In Jesus name, Amen.*

My Heart Note

(Take this time to write any note of reflection, personal takeaway, or note to the Father)

YOU ARE PRECIOUS AND HONORED IN MY EYES

Day 15

"Since you are precious and honored in my sight and because I love you, I will give people in exchange for you, nations in exchange for your life."
Isaiah 43:4 (NIV)

My devotion, faithfulness, and commitment to you will always be demonstrated not just with my thoughts or words, but my actions toward you throughout time. My sacrificial love displayed unto you is not just by action, it simply is who I am, for I am love. As your God, as your Father, there is nothing that can separate you from my love. I know you have experienced love that's conditional, but my love is unconditional. You don't have to earn my love my daughter, you just have to receive it. Because you are mine and I love you, I will cause my favor to rest upon you. I will defend you, deliver you from the hand of the enemy and I will fight for you. You are precious in my eyes daughter.

***Prayer**: Father, I thank you that I am honored and precious in your sight. I thank you for your love that sustains me, fights for me, defends me, and protects me. In the moments that I experience injustice, accusation, unfairness, and accusation, may I be reminded that you will vindicate me, and may I relinquish the desire to defend myself. In Jesus' name, Amen.*

My Heart Note

(Take this time to write any note of reflection, personal takeaway, or note to the Father)

I TAKE DELIGHT IN YOU

Day 16

"The Lord your God is with you, the Mighty Warrior who saves. He will take great delight in you; in His love, He will no longer rebuke you, but will rejoice over you with singing."
Zephaniah 3:17 (NIV)

I find great pleasure and joy in you. As I see my word accomplished in your life. You are in the palm of my hand and nothing or no one can pluck you out of it. In the midst of chaos, and uncertainty I sing over you with sounds of healing, peace, joy, and happiness. It is my hope that you receive my words in a fresh way today. In the current season that you're in may you come to know and experience me as the Mighty Warrior, one who will fight for you. I am not here to reprimand you but rejoice over you.

Prayer: *Father I thank you for protecting me, and for guiding me. May the songs of rejoicing that you sing over me refresh me in times of obscurity. May your love and delight in me bring comfort to my soul. In* Jesus' name, Amen.

My Heart Note

(Take this time to write any note of reflection, personal takeaway, or note to the Father)

YOU ARE CHOSEN AND HOLY

Day 17

"For he chose us in him before the creation of the world to be holy and blameless in his sight."
Ephesians 1:4 (NIV)

Before the earth was formed, I made a conscious decision, I sought you out and I chose you for myself. I wanted you, I set you apart to be Holy. Not demanding your servitude in your own strength to be Holy. You are Holy because you are in me, and I am Holy. I set you apart from my purposes, to demonstrate my glory through you. I love to take the ones that people deem as nobodies as I make them not just somebodies but powerful vessels that carry my anointing. If you're still not sure, I chose you as my daughter. I chose you for such as a time as this. You don't have to perform to be Holy or chosen, you already are through me; now just be.

***Prayer**: Father, I thank you that you chose me and predestined me to be Holy. I am Holy because you are Holy. I release the impulse to "perform" to be Holy or even prove myself to be chosen; to myself, to you, and to others. I thank you Father that even when I don't always get it right, you don't find fault. For when you see me you see me unblemished, righteous, virtuous, and blameless. I choose this day forward to walk in the confidence of how you see me. Thank you for choosing me. In Jesus' name, Amen.*

My Heart Note

(Take this time to write any note of reflection, personal takeaway, or note to the Father)

YOU ARE SEATED IN THE HEAVENLY PLACES WITH CHRIST

Day 18

"And he raised us up with him and seated us with him in the heavenly realms in Christ Jesus."
Ephesians 2:6 (NIV)

The life you live now is in Jesus Christ. You share in his death burial and resurrection. When Christ arose you arose as well, and sin no longer has a hold on you; your life is lived vertically with Him. Just as He is seated at my right hand you are seated as well my daughter. Your spiritual position is seated in the heavenlies. You live from a place of victory. There will be many things you encounter while on earth that will challenge your spiritual position. May you live in a way that reveres your position in Christ and brings glory to Me.

***Prayer**: Father I thank you that I am seated with Christ in heavenly places. It is by your grace and not of any merit of my own. I thank you that my spiritual position cannot be taken away from me. Help me, Father, to continue to renew my mind, and live this life by faith and from my heavenly position. In Jesus' name, Amen.*

My Heart Note

(Take this time to write any note of reflection, personal takeaway, or note to the Father)

YOU ARE MY WORKMANSHIP CREATED TO PRODUCE GOOD WORKS

Day 19

"For we are his workmanship, having been created in Christ Jesus for good works that God prepared beforehand so we may do them."
Ephesians 2:10 (NET)

Your essential design, my overall purpose outlined for you, is to produce good works. I prepared you and designed you beforehand to walk in the things I have created for you. I gave you the capacity to produce although at times you question your ability. As you trust me with your adequacy, competency, and efficiency of your creation you will freely produce without fear. You were crafted with skill and purpose to show forth my redemptive and purifying hand.

***Prayer**: Father, I thank you that you crafted me with skill and purpose for your purposes. I submit my will to yours. Even while feeling incompetent, unskilled, and unqualified may I rest in the finished work that you created me for good works. In Jesus's name, Amen.*

My Heart Note

(Take this time to write any note of reflection, personal takeaway, or note to the Father)

YOU ARE A CITIZEN OF HEAVEN

Day 20

"But our citizenship is in heaven--and we also await a savior from there, the Lord Jesus Christ."
Philippians 3:20 (ESV)

Your time here is but a vapor, as eternity awaits in the distance with Me. You are not of this world, for your citizenship is in Heaven. Therefore, the persecution, afflictions, and trials you encounter on your journey on earth are temporary, but your home that waits for your return is forever. Remember my daughter, only what you do for Me will last. There will be mountaintop and valley experiences but take heart, my child, this too shall pass. May you find comfort in knowing that I, the Savior will come. As you patiently wait for My return don't become consumed with the way of living here, may your light shine before all men, may you do all that I have called you to do, and may you find joy in knowing that your home in its tranquil nature, has been prepared.

***Prayer**: Father, I thank you that I am a citizen of Heaven. I am in the world but not of the world so I set my affection on things above. This earth shall pass away and the cares and sufferings of this life cannot be compared to the glory that will be revealed to me. Father, help me be the light that will draw others to you. Let my faith and hope in you draw others to you, so they too can share in the eternal reward. In Jesus' name, Amen.*

My Heart Note

(Take this time to write any note of reflection, personal takeaway, or note to the Father)

YOU ARE PROTECTED

Day 21

"He will not let your foot slip, he who watches over you will not slumber;"
Psalms 121:3 (NIV)

In a world infused with fear, as my child, you can find security in Me. I give my angels charge over you to keep you in all your ways. In your coming in and in your going out I will ensure your safety because of my love and care for you. I am with you, my daughter, every step of the way. While it's hard to see your way, and the steps you're taking; know that I am guiding your feet. When your journey gets rocky and even slippery and it feels like you are about to lose your way, I am there to place your feet back on course. Even when you may be blindsided, I am there to rescue you. For I am with you, protecting and watching over you day and night. I will not slumber for you are mine and I will protect you at all cost. You are mine.

***Prayer**: Father, I thank you that you are protecting and watching over me to ensure that I am safe. I close the door to fear and command its grip to loose every area in my life where I have tried to protect myself. I am safe in you and there is safety in your love. I receive your perfect love today that casts out fear. In Jesus' name, Amen.*

My Heart Note

(Take this time to write any note of reflection, personal takeaway, or note to the Father)

YOU ARE PREDESTINED

Day 22

"For those God foreknew he also predestined to be conformed to the image of his Son, that he might be the firstborn among many brothers and sisters."

Romans 8:29 (NIV)

I saw you from afar off my daughter. I foreknew that you would believe in my son. I chose you and destined your very life to be conformed to image of my son, Jesus. I was certain about my election then, I'm sure of my election now and I will still be sure about my election later. I know there are moments when you are unsure of yourself at times; but may I remind you that I chose you before the foundation of the world. Your status, your job title, your level of education, etc. are irrelevant factors. I chose you not by what the world values but by what is valuable, and that is you. I'm not asking for your perfectionism, just your surrendered obedience to My Will for your life for it has been predestined.

***Prayer**: Father, I thank you that you have preordained and predestined my life in Jesus Christ. I submit my fears, anxiety, and uncertainty to you. I put off striving for perfection and clothe myself with the grace that you have given me to walk out what has been predestined for my life. In Jesus' name, Amen.*

My Heart Note

(Take this time to write any note of reflection, personal takeaway, or note to the Father)

YOU ARE IMPORTANT

Day 23

"But you are a chosen people, a royal priesthood, a holy nation, God's special possession, that you may declare the praises of him who called you out of darkness into his wonderful light."
1 Peter 2:9 (NIV)

I sought you out, I called you out of darkness, out of the snare of the hand of the enemy and his deception. You are mine, one of royal heritage, set apart for my purposes. You were created as a beacon of light to shine within dark places. You were never designed to blend in but to Illuminate every space you encounter. You are my special people, one that I have called unto myself and one that has responded to the call. Continue to respond through your faith my daughter, offering your life as a living sacrifice unto me.

***Prayer:** Father I praise you for calling me out of darkness and into your marvelous light. May my life be a living sacrifice: pure, holy, and acceptable unto you. I thank you for your Holy Spirit that enables me to walk as a child of the light. May your light continue to shine through me so that I may draw others to you. In Jesus' name, Amen.*

My Heart Note

(Take this time to write any note of reflection, personal takeaway, or note to the Father)

YOU ARE GIFTED

Day 24

"Every good and perfect gift is from above, coming down from the Father of the heavenly lights, who does not change like shifting shadows."

James 1:17 (KJV)

I am a good Father that gives good gifts. Every good and perfect gift comes from me. It is not in my nature to give bad, imperfect, faulty, or destructive gifts. However, many have become entangled in the lies of the enemy that cause one to look at oneself as the provider of the gift. The gifts are just gifts and should not be worshipped but rather used to point back to Me, the One who gave it. My daughter, I have good gifts that I want to give you. My gift-giving isn't predicated on how good you are or how awful you think you are at times. Because you are my child and belong to me, I yearn to give you great gifts. I will not go back or refrain from giving you what I have spoken to you for every promise of mine is yes and amen and every word I've spoken to you shall be fulfilled.

***Prayer**: Father I thank you that every good and perfect give comes from you. I thank you that you freely give and you are not hesitant to give me good gifts. I receive every gift you have given me. I will use your gifts you placed within me for your glory and will not let fear or accusation from the enemy cause me to reject, shrink back or idolize the gifts. Father, help me to remain focused on you and not become consumed with the gifts you give, but honor you through them. In Jesus' Name, Amen.*

My Heart Note

(Take this time to write any note of reflection, personal takeaway, or note to the Father)

YOUR WORDS HAVE POWER

Day 25

"Thou shalt also decree a thing, and it shall be established unto thee: and the light shall shine upon thy ways."
Job 22:28 (KJV)

Whatever has been dead in your life, whatever has been barren, I have given you the authority to resurrect it by the power that lies within speaking My Word. No matter how long you have been in a situation that has been dry, lifeless, and unfertile; I want you to continue to speak life, my daughter. May your tongue be the nutrients to the desert places in your life. May your words align with My Word. Stand boldly my daughter to proclaim, declare, and decree what you want to see and I will see to it to cause my light to shine upon all of your ways!

***Prayer**: Father, I thank you that I can exercise the dominion and authority that you have given me by speaking your Word over any situation in my life. As I decree and declare your word it shall be so! You will cause your light to shine upon whatever I do and wherever I am. In Jesus' Name, Amen.*

My Heart Note

(Take this time to write any note of reflection, personal takeaway, or note to the Father)

YOU ARE THE HEAD AND NOT THE TAIL

Day 26

"The Lord will make you the head, not the tail. If you pay attention to the commands of the Lord your God that I give you this day and carefully follow them, you will always be at the top, never at the bottom."

Deuteronomy 28:13 (NIV)

I have designed you as my child to live a life as one who belongs and represents my Kingdom. The principles of the Kingdom of Heaven is designed for you to live a life of freedom within Me and not in bondage like a slave. For the world system teaches you how to maintain and self-sustain; But I the Sustainer will cause you to never be in lack, need, falling behind, or at the bottom. Even if you are experiencing that now may you find hope in knowing that I have a better way for you and you don't have to stay where you are. This way has been made available to you as you live by the Spirit and heed My voice.

***Prayer**: Father, I thank you that you have designed me to be the head and not the tail as I am intentional about following you, doing your word, and being led by your Spirit. I call forth the power of the Holy Spirit to begin to tear down the walls of the Babylonian system within my mind so that It may receive the Kingdom principles and apply them to my life. For I declare I am the head and not the tail. In Jesus' Name. Amen*

My Heart Note

(Take this time to write any note of reflection, personal takeaway, or note to the Father)

I WILL NOT LEAVE OR FORSAKE YOU

Day 27

" Be strong and courageous. Do not fear or be in dread of them, for it is the LORD your God who goes with you. He will not leave you or forsake you."

Hebrews 13:6 (ESV)

The strength and courage needed for the journey were never intended to be fueled or sustained by you alone. I, the Greater One has gone before you and I have conquered it. You will go through trials, testing and troubles. But even in the midst of the storms, the winds, the fire, and the waters; I will be with you You will face persecution, but dare not be afraid for I go with you, not just as your God but as your Father. The one who loves you, the one who cares. I am with you, my daughter. I will never leave you to fend for yourself. I am your protector, I am your vindicator. Be strong my daughter and take heart for I am with you.

***Prayer**: Father I thank you that you are with me every step of my journey. You will never leave me or forsake me. I call forth the boldness of the Lord to arise within me and courage as I stand and advance forward in the midst of adversity, trials, and persecution. I thank you Father for you have not given me a spirit of fear but of power, love, and a sound mind. In Jesus' Name. Amen.*

My Heart Note

(Take this time to write any note of reflection, personal takeaway, or note to the Father)

I LOVE YOU WITH AN EVERLASTING LOVE

Day 28

"Long ago the LORD said to Israel: "I have loved you, my people, with an everlasting love. With unfailing love, I have drawn you to myself."

Jeremiah 31:3 (NLT)

My love for you stretches from the beginning of time throughout all eternity. My love was preordained for you. My heart flutters as I think about the day when I formed you within your mother's womb. You my creation, my daughter, the love I have for you is eternal. My love for you will never change. On your journey, you will encounter people, even those whom you love that will walk away from you, reject you, disown you, and fail you. I, my daughter, will NEVER fail you, leave you, reject you, or walk away from you. I desired you even before your existence came to be. I've drawn you to myself for eternity. May you find comfort and peace in knowing that I, your God, your Father, am with you. Receive my love for youfrom this day forward. Let my love quiet your fears, your doubts, and your soul.

***Prayer**: Father, reveal the places within me where I have put boundaries and safeguards up within myself to keep from experiencing hurt. For you have come to heal the brokenhearted and bind up their wombs. Reveal Father as I allow myself to become vulnerable and undone in you. From this day forward may I come to know and receive your love in a greater way. In Jesus' Name, Amen.*

My Heart Note

(Take this time to write any note of reflection, personal takeaway, or note to the Father)